Flash Revise
Pocketbook

A2 Economics

Philip Allan Updates, an imprint of Hodder Education, an Hachette UK company, Market Place, Deddington, Oxfordshire OX15 0SE

Orders

Bookpoint Ltd, 130 Milton Park, Abingdon, Oxfordshire OX14 4SB
tel: 01235 827720   fax: 01235 400454   e-mail: uk.orders@bookpoint.co.uk

Lines are open 9.00 a.m.–5.00 p.m., Monday to Saturday, with a 24-hour message answering service. You can also order through our website: www.philipallan.co.uk

Printed in Spain

Hachette UK's policy is to use papers that are natural, renewable and recyclable products and made from wood grown in sustainable forests. The logging and manufacturing processes are expected to conform to the environmental regulations of the country of origin.

P01557

Microeconomics

1 Contestability
2 Barriers to entry
3 Pareto efficiency/optimality
4 Economic efficiency
5 X-inefficiency
6 Costs of production
7 Costs in the long run
8 Satisficing
9 Divorcing ownership from control
10 Predatory pricing
11 Price making/taking
12 Perfect competition
13 Equilibrium for a perfectly competitive firm
14 Monopolistic competition
15 Product differentiation
16 Profit maximising equilibrium in monopolistic competition
17 Excess capacity
18 Oligopoly
19 Kinked demand curve
20 Collusion
21 Game theory
22 Monopoly
23 Equilibrium for a monopolistic firm
24 Concentration ratio
25 Deadweight loss
26 Price discrimination
27 Monopoly profit
28 Multinational corporation (MNC)
29 Public–private partnership
30 Deregulation
31 Privatisation
32 Utility regulator
33 Sustainable transport system
34 Transport modes
35 Congestion cost
36 Road pricing
37 Integrated transport policy
38 Labour mobility
39 Marginal physical product
40 Marginal revenue productivity
41 Equilibrium wage rate
42 Supply of labour curve
43 Supply of effort curve
44 Labour market elasticity
45 Economic rent
46 Transfer earning
47 Monopsony buyer of labour
48 National minimum wage (NMW)
49 Collective bargaining
50 Equal Pay Act (EPA)

Macroeconomics

Contestability

Q1 A perfectly contestable market has no s_____ c_____.

Q2 Explain how an industry with only a few firms could be contestable.

Q3 Explain the relationship between 'hit and run' and contestability.

Q4 If there is greater contestability, are firms more likely to make normal or abnormal profits in the long run?

ANSWERS ▶▶

a measure of the degree of difficulty firms have in entering and leaving an industry

A1 *sunk costs*

A2 as long as there are potential entrants into the industry, prices will be kept down by the threat of more competition

A3 zero sunk costs produce costless entry and exit into and out of the industry, allowing competitive firms to hit (enter) and run (exit)

A4 greater contestability will push firms towards normal profits in the long run

***examiner's* note** In market theory, contestability transcends the accepted divisions between traditional theories of the firm. A recognition that markets can be made more or less contestable by the actions of government should shift the emphasis of competition policy away from rigidly prescribed numbers such as 25% penetration towards the idea of creating and maintaining contestability in markets irrespective of the size of the firm and the industry's concentration ratio.

 ANSWERS

Barriers to entry

Q1 What barrier to entry is illustrated in the diagram?

Q2 Identify a profit-maximising equilibrium.

Q3 Which equilibrium will produce allocative efficiency?

Q4 Why would this firm be unable to sustain allocative efficiency?

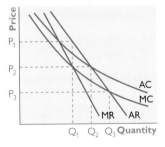

A1 persistently falling unit costs will produce a natural monopoly and a natural barrier

A2 P_1Q_1 is the profit-maximising equilibrium where MC = MR

A3 P = MC produces allocative efficiency and that equilibrium is at P_3Q_3

A4 an allocatively efficient equilibrium produces a loss as AR is below AC

***examiner's* note** A natural monopoly results from a situation where the total market demand is satisfied while the average and marginal cost curves are still falling. This usually occurs as the result of technical economies of scale. Privatisation created the potential for some firms to become natural monopolies and, in order to stop excessive profit making, regulators were established to control the pricing policies of newly privatised industries.

 ANSWERS

Pareto efficiency/optimality

Q1 Who was Pareto?

Q2 What does an optimal distribution of products to consumers require?

Q3 What does an optimal allocation of factors to production require?

Q4 What is the price of a product equal to when an optimal output occurs?

ANSWERS

when it is not possible to make anyone better off without making someone else worse off

A1 Vilfredo Pareto (1848–1923) was an Italian economist who introduced the mathematical formulation for an optimum allocation of resources

A2 an equalisation of marginal utilities per unit of money spent by consumers on a variety of products

A3 an equalisation of marginal products per unit of money spent by producers on different productive factors

A4 the marginal cost of producing the last unit of a product

***examiner's* note** The optimal conditions required are highly theoretical and unobtainable in reality. However, they apply a useful benchmark to analysing resource allocation. In contrast, an analysis of policies that involve the redirection of resources often looks at the costs to some members of the community and the benefits to others of supporting a redistribution of resources.

(**3**) **ANSWERS**

Economic efficiency

Q1 What is productive efficiency?

Q2 What is allocative efficiency?

Q3 On the diagram, which equilibrium produces excess capacity?

Q4 If D shifts to D_1, are both efficiencies likely to be observed?

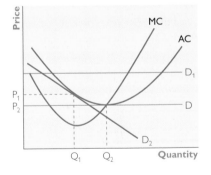

includes conditions of productive and allocative efficiency and sometimes refers to dynamic efficiency

A1 where firms are producing at the lowest point on the average cost curve

A2 where the price of the product sold to consumers is equal to the marginal cost of producing the last product

A3 P_1Q_1 is a monopolistically competitive equilibrium where the firm produces below optimum size and unit costs are not at a minimum

A4 no; if the firm is profit maximising, P will equal MC but the firm will be over optimum size

***examiner's* note** Perfect competition produces allocative efficiency in both the short and long run and productive efficiency in the long run. The other theories of the firm produce both allocative and productive inefficiency. Dynamic efficiency refers to a situation where the activities of a firm can shift the cost curves down over time. Usually a significant spend on R&D increases dynamic efficiency.

 ANSWERS

X-inefficiency

Q1 What is y-inefficiency?

Q2 What is the difference between x- and y-inefficiency?

Q3 Why were nationalised industries accused of being x-inefficient?

Q4 Both types of inefficiency can occur in the p............ or p............ sector of the economy and they both assume a d............ of i............ on the part of the producer.

ANSWERS

when a firm's average cost curve is not at its lowest attainable level

A1 when a firm with significant market power and little or no competition has become lax about market opportunities and the potential for new customers

A2 x-inefficiency deals with current costs; y-inefficiency deals with potential revenues

A3 they were judged to be inefficient in the way that they coordinated and controlled their work practices

A4 *public; private; degree; incompetence*

***examiner's* note** In microeconomic analysis, studies of efficiency and inefficiency are very important. The theoretical extremes of productive, allocative, dynamic and Pareto efficiency are rarely, if ever, achievable in reality, while inefficiencies abound as the result of imperfect knowledge, lack of competition and lack of motivation.

(5) **ANSWERS**

Costs of production

Q1 Identify the short-run curves A, B, C and D.

Q2 What is the difference between the short run and long run?

Q3 Do average fixed costs fall, or fall and rise, or remain constant?

Q4 What is the distance between A and B the same as?

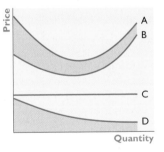

ANSWERS

A1 A = average total cost; B = average variable cost; C = total fixed cost; D = average fixed cost

A2 short run includes at least one fixed factor; in the long run all factors are variable

A3 they continue to fall towards zero at infinity

A4 D and zero

***examiner's* note** The costs of employing land, labour, capital and enterprise make up the costs of producing goods and services. In the very short run (momentary period) all productive factors are fixed and therefore costs are also fixed. In the short run only variable costs change while in the long run all factors are variable and hence so are costs. In the very long run costs can be reduced at the same level of output as the result of technology no longer being considered a constant.

Microeconomics

Costs in the long run

Q1 What is the long run?

Q2 What causes the shape
(a) between X and Y?
(b) between Y and Z?

Q3 Describe the points of
tangency between the
curves.

Q4 Point Y is the m............ e............
s............

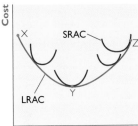

ANSWERS

A1 that time period when all productive factors are variable

A2 (a) X to Y = economies of scale
(b) Y to Z = diseconomies of scale

A3 in each case, as both curves have the same slope where they touch, only at position Y can the point of tangency be at the lowest point on both curves

A4 *minimum efficient scale*

***examiner's* note** There is an important distinction between, on the one hand, increasing and diminishing marginal returns, where the short-run constraint requires variable factors to be added to fixed factors, and on the other, the increasing and diminishing returns to scale that occur in the long run when all the productive factors can be changed in the same proportions. Note that, as illustrated in the diagram on the other side of this card, the long-run average cost curve is often referred to as an envelope around the short-run cost curves.

 **ANSWERS**

Satisficing

Q1 What is the rule for a profit-maximising firm?

Q2 Why may a firm choose sales revenue maximisation rather than profit maximisation as its target?

Q3 Sales revenue maximisation expands the output of a firm up to the point where m............ r............ is z............ .

Q4 If a firm chooses sales maximisation rather than revenue maximisation, how far could it expand and still remain profitable?

ANSWERS

an action sufficient to satisfy the economic agent but that does not result in maximising behaviour

A1 profits are maximised where marginal cost equals marginal revenue

A2 the divorce of ownership from control means that managers are likely to expand the business to boost their salaries, given a satisfactory level of profits

A3 *marginal revenue*; zero (after this point, sales revenue falls, as marginal revenue is negative)

A4 up to the point where total revenue equals total cost and normal profits are achieved

***examiner's* note** Most theories of a firm's behaviour are based on the assumption that firms aim to profit maximise. However, alternative objectives may play a part in determining behaviour. Sufficient levels of profit to satisfy shareholders may allow firms to increase their size in pursuit of status and market dominance.

Divorcing ownership from control

Q1 Who owns a public limited company (plc)?

Q2 Why would managers prefer Q_2 to Q_1?

Q3 What is the restriction on how far to expand?

Q4 In what way can managers be made more responsive to profits?

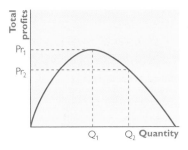

ANSWERS

occurs in large companies where the owners are not the managers of the company

A1 shareholders who usually have little knowledge of the company

A2 often managers' salaries relate to the size of the firm and their level of responsibility, both of which are increased at output Q_2

A3 it is important to earn a sufficient level of profits to satisfy the shareholders

A4 they can be forced to be shareholders who depend on dividends for a significant part of their income

***examiner's* note** Shareholder meetings of plcs are attended by a minute proportion of the total shareholders and the annual reports are read by a similar number. Because shareholders are often only interested in dividend pay-outs, the managers are less concerned with profit maximisation and more interested in the size and status of the company. As a manager's salary is likely to be linked to the turnover of the company, there is a tendency for expansionary decision making.

 **9** **ANSWERS**

Predatory pricing

Q1 Give an example of how a supermarket may use predatory pricing on some of its products.

Q2 Why is a predatory price unsustainable in the long run?

Q3 What is the difference between predatory pricing and limit pricing?

Q4 Why is predatory pricing more likely to occur in large firms with diversified product ranges?

ANSWERS

where a firm charges loss-making prices in order to force a competitor out of the market

A1 loss-making prices may be used on products placed near the entrance to attract customers into the shop

A2 it is a loss-making price and can only be used for a short period

A3 predatory pricing is designed to force competitors out of a market; limit pricing is used to stop firms entering a market

A4 large firms can cross-subsidise their loss-making products from profits on their other products

***examiner's* note** Supermarkets may argue that they are using competitive prices rather than predatory prices, but it has long been accepted that a supermarket is selling a basket of goods to its customers and not just one product. The cheap products encourage the customers in and then they have to walk through aisles of other products before they leave the store.

Price making/taking

Q1 What behaviour is most influential in determining whether a firm takes a price?

Q2 Can a monopolist determine both the price and output of its product?

Q3 What is the relationship between price making/taking and collusion in an oligopolistic market?

Q4 Does a monopolistically competitive firm make or take a price?

ANSWERS ▶▶

A1 the degree of competitive behaviour

A2 no, a monopolist can determine either price or output, but not both

A3 collusion allows a number of firms to make a price; lack of collusion leads them to take a price

A4 it takes a price as there are lots of competitive firms and no barriers to entry

***examiner's* note** Given high levels of competition or contestability, individual firms are assumed not to be able to influence price. They must accept the market price or be forced out of business. As a market structure moves closer to monopoly, so it becomes possible to erect barriers and establish a price that allows supernormal profits to be maintained in the long term.

(11) ANSWERS

Perfect competition

Q1 Explain what is meant by the statement, 'competitive firms are price takers'.

Q2 Perfectly competitive firms produce h............ products and sell in markets that have p............ k............ .

Q3 Give an example of a market that comes close to perfect competition.

Q4 In a more competitive industry, is the concentration ratio higher or lower?

ANSWERS

an industry comprising many buyers and many small, identical firms

A1 each firm supplies such a small part of the total market that it cannot influence the market price

A2 *homogeneous; perfect knowledge*

A3 examples include the foreign exchange market, cereal crops and milk

A4 the concentration ratio for three firms in a more competitive industry is lower, e.g. 2%, while that for a less competitive industry is higher, e.g. 70%

***examiner's* note** In real life the assumptions made about a perfectly competitive industry (i.e. homogeneous products, perfect knowledge and total freedom of movement) may never apply or never apply simultaneously. It must be emphasised that these assumptions produce an extreme model, which is primarily an analytical device to allow students of the subject to reach a certain level of basic understanding.

Equilibrium for a perfectly competitive firm

Q1 At what point does long-run equilibrium occur?

Q2 At what point does short-run equilibrium occur?

Q3 Which curve(s) represent(s) marginal revenue and average revenue?

Q4 The distance between which two curves represents excessive profits?

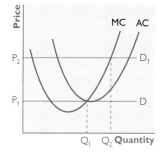

ANSWERS 》

the profit-maximising equilibrium occurs where marginal revenue = marginal cost (rising)

A1 at the point of tangency between D and AC, where marginal cost = marginal revenue and normal profit is achieved

A2 at the point of intersection between D_1 and MC, where marginal cost = marginal revenue and excessive profit is achieved

A3 D_1 and D both represent marginal revenue and average revenue when the demand curve is perfectly elastic

A4 the distance between average cost and average revenue (D_1)

***examiner's* note** The theory of perfect competition is an extremely simplified model based on a number of unrealistic assumptions such as homogeneous products and perfect knowledge. This lack of realism results from the need to produce an easily understood model on which a foundation of knowledge can be built. From this position, more complex models can be constructed and analysed.

Monopolistic competition

Q1 What is product differentiation?

Q2 What does the word 'monopolistic' refer to in 'monopolistic competition'?

Q3 Why can monopolistically competitive firms make excessive profits only in the short run?

Q4 A successful advertising campaign is likely to have two effects on the demand curve for a product. What are they?

ANSWERS ▶▶

an industry with many firms producing similar, but not identical, products

A1 where the firm tries to make a product different, or seem different, from its competitors' product

A2 it refers to a monopolistic control over the name and brand image of a competitive product

A3 in the long run, excessive profits will be eroded by new firms entering the industry

A4 it will shift the demand curve to the right and make demand for the product more inelastic as it becomes resistant to price rises

***examiner's* note** Monopolistic competition is closer to reality than perfect competition. It still has many firms, but they work hard through advertising to create an image for their product that separates them from their competitors. Many industries are made up of monopolistically competitive firms.

Product differentiation

Q1 Does product differentiation take place in perfect competition?

Q2 What effect does successful product differentiation have on price elasticity of demand?

Q3 What is meant by 'branding' a product?

Q4 Why do firms compete with themselves through brand proliferation and offer differentiated versions of a similar product, e.g. washing powder?

ANSWERS

A1 no, because products are assumed to be homogeneous and consumers have perfect knowledge

A2 it makes the products more price inelastic as consumers are less responsive to price changes

A3 the creation of an image for a product, usually through advertising, that differentiates it from similar products in the market place

A4 this increases the size of the market for the product by targeting segments that demand slightly different characteristics

***examiner's* note** Product differentiation is a realistic interpretation of the world of business, where each firm is trying to create an impression in the mind of the consumer that its product is unique. In order to do this, firms often use a large marketing budget and reinforce their image continuously.

(15) ANSWERS

Profit maximising equilibrium in monopolistic competition

Q1 Why are the words 'monopoly' and 'competition' included in this description of a firm?

Q2 Which demand curve produces a long-run equilibrium?

Q3 Given long-run equilibrium, where does MR intersect MC?

Q4 What is the relationship between product differentiation and PED?

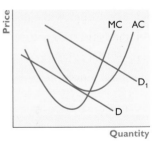

ANSWERS

A1 the monopoly is over an image, brand or name while the firm
is competing with many other similar firms

A2 D, as it is tangent to AC and consistent with normal profits

A3 directly below the point of tangency between D and AC

A4 the more differentiated the product, the more inelastic the
demand curve

***examiner's* note** Monopolistic competition is more realistic than perfect
competition as it recognises the motivation that each firm has to try to make its
product seem different from similar competing products. This tends to mean that
marketing and advertising play an important role in trying to create a brand
image that concentrates on differences rather than similarities between products.

Excess capacity

Q1 In which industry will firms have excess capacity in the long run: monopoly, monopolistic competition, perfect competition?

Q2 A firm producing at capacity output is also said to be of an o............ s............ .

Q3 Will a firm with excess capacity increase or decrease its average cost when it expands its output?

Q4 Is a firm with excess capacity likely to have a lower price and a higher output than a firm producing at full capacity?

ANSWERS

when a firm is producing a level of output less than that required to achieve minimum average cost

A1 only in monopolistic competition will a firm always have excess capacity in the long run

A2 *optimum size*; this is also at the lowest point on the average cost curve

A3 average cost will decrease as output expands

A4 no; it is likely to have a higher price and a lower output

examiner's note Firms in monopolistic competition will always have any of their excessive profits removed through competition. This means that the addition to revenue from selling one more product will always equal the addition to costs of producing one more product at a level of output which is less than that required to minimise unit costs.

 **ANSWERS**

Oligopoly

Q1 Why might oligopolistic firms be attracted to collusion?

Q2 Why is the demand curve for an oligopolistic firm kinked at the prevailing market price?

Q3 Why might oligopolistic firms be more interested in non-price competition?

Q4 What is a business strategy based upon brand proliferation?

ANSWERS

an imperfect market structure comprising a few large firms

A1 it is possible, but not legal, for a few firms to make higher profits through collusive decisions

A2 if any one firm raises price, it will lose a lot of orders to competitors, whereas if it lowers price, other firms will copy, so as not to lose orders

A3 to increase market share, when pricing policies are not successful

A4 a firm may try to increase market share by creating different brands with marginal differences in product specification, e.g. soap powders

***examiner's* note** Oligopolists have an incentive to work together for mutual benefit and may make overt or covert agreements on price, output, market separation and advertising. Legally, there are limits to the extent that firms can collude, as it is arguably to the benefit of the consumer if competitive forces erode excessive profits by forcing down price and encouraging an expansion in output.

Kinked demand curve

Q1 Which type of firm faces a kinked demand curve?

Q2 Given P_1, what happens to revenue and sales when price is raised or lowered?

Q3 Is the industry demand curve kinked?

Q4 Why is the demand curve price inelastic below P_1?

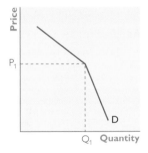

ANSWERS ▶▶

the curve is kinked at the prevailing market price
and is elastic above P_1 and inelastic below P_1

A1 an oligopolistic firm

A2 a rise in price reduces sales and revenue; a fall in price increases sales but reduces revenue

A3 no, only the firm's demand curve is assumed to be kinked

A4 if a firm lowers price, then other firms will follow suit and each firm will only receive a share of the increased market demand

***examiner's* note** An oligopoly includes a few large firms in an industry, each with a large market share. The result is that, if any firm raises price independently of the other firms, it loses a significant number of potential sales. If it decides to lower price, then the other firms will follow immediately so as not to lose market share and the result is only a small increase in sales as the total market expands at lower prices.

(19) ANSWERS

Collusion

Q1 Is an oligopolistic or a monopolistically competitive industry more likely to attempt collusion?

Q2 What are the advantages of collusion?

Q3 If both collusion and competition cause all firms to sell at the same price, why is there so much concern about collusion?

Q4 What is the difference between tacit and formal collusion?

ANSWERS

an agreement between firms to avoid damaging each other by individual price, output or marketing decisions

A1 a few firms in an oligopolistic industry may attempt collusion, whereas it is impractical for many firms to collude

A2 it allows firms to reduce output, raise price and make excessive profits in the long run

A3 the collusive price will be higher than the competitive price

A4 tacit collusion is informal; a formal collusion agreement involves sanctions for non-compliance

***examiner's* note** The more firms there are in an industry the less likely it is that collusion will be successful. Collusion usually benefits producers to the disadvantage of consumers. For example, a price agreement between a few firms is generally led by the least efficient firm and prices will be higher than the competitive price. More efficient firms benefit with higher profits and less efficient firms at least stay in business. This situation has been outlawed by legislation as an anti-competitive practice.

 **ANSWERS**

Game theory

Q1 Which structure for an industry uses a game theory explanation?

Q2 Which combination in the matrix is likely to produce excessive profits?

Q3 Which combination is likely to produce a loss for firm Y?

Q4 Which combination is likely to produce normal profits?

	Firm X	
	Comply	Cheat
Comply	A	B
Firm Y		
Cheat	C	D

ANSWERS

explains outcomes when rational decisions are based on gauging the reaction of competitors

A1 oligopolistic industries have few enough firms to be able to collude in an essentially competitive environment

A2 combination A, if the collusion is successful

A3 combination B where firm Y agrees to collusion but X cheats and forces Y into a loss-making situation

A4 combination D is equivalent to both firms competing away any excessive profits

***examiner's* note** Game theory is based on the mathematics of John Forbes Nash whose life is portrayed in the film *A Beautiful Mind*. In reality firms have every incentive, in a competitive environment, to protect their knowledge and act in ways that surprise their competitors. Textbooks generally suggest that a duopoly is most likely to collude to make excessive profits. However, game theory predicts that because neither firm is certain about the other's action they will be forced to compete away excessive profits.

Monopoly

Q1 Can a monopolist control the price and quantity of a product supplied to the market?

Q2 How do legal monopolies and theoretical monopolies differ?

Q3 To maintain monopoly power, a firm needs b............ to e............ into the market.

Q4 If total market demand is satisfied when technical economies of scale are still reducing costs, explain what type of market structure exists.

ANSWERS

an industry where one firm has control over supply and can maintain control in the long run

A1 a monopolist can only control either price or quantity, but not both

A2 a legal monopoly is defined as a firm having control over 25% or more of the market, whereas a theoretical monopoly is just one firm

A3 *barriers to entry* (necessary to block competitors)

A4 a natural monopoly, as one firm will always be more efficient than two or more firms

***examiner's* note** As a sole producer, the monopolist has total control over the supply of the product and, as such, is a price maker. The monopolist has no power to dictate demand, but is able to discover the nature of demand and then offer the quantity that will yield the largest profit. Monopolies can be formed naturally without any deliberate action on the part of the producer, or they can be contrived to benefit either the producer or consumer.

Equilibrium for a monopolistic firm

Q1 Which equilibrium is profit maximising?

Q2 Which equilibrium is allocatively efficient?

Q3 Which combination of price and quantity is not an equilibrium?

Q4 Which equilibrium produces normal profits?

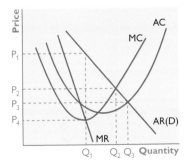

A1 P_1Q_1 is established by a quantity where $MC = MR$ and the price
is raised to a profit-maximising level determined by demand

A2 an equilibrium where $P = MC$ at P_2Q_2 is allocatively efficient

A3 P_4Q_1 is not an equilibrium as supply is less than demand

A4 P_3Q_3 is where $AC = AR$

***examiner's* note** A common mistake is to identify P_4Q_1 as a profit-maximising
equilibrium, but it is not an equilibrium as supply does not equal demand and,
although Q_1 is the profit-maximising output, it is the price P_1 that maximises
profits. Equilibriums occur at any point where supply = demand and it is only the
assumption, i.e. profit maximising or sales revenue maximising (where MR is 0),
that produces a unique position in the model.

(23) **ANSWERS**

Concentration ratio

Q1 In what way might concentration ratios suggest market imperfection?

Q2 Firm A has 20% of the market, firm B has 35% and firm C has 25%. What is the three-firm concentration ratio?

Q3 If a three-firm concentration ratio was 73%, why might the Monopolies Commission show an interest?

Q4 Is it possible for a contestable market to have a concentration ratio of 90%?

ANSWERS

a percentage measure of total market sales achieved by a specified number of firms in that market

A1 the higher the concentration ratio, the closer to oligopoly and monopoly structures

A2 80% of total market sales are made by the three firms

A3 at least one of the firms must supply 25% or more of the total market by sales

A4 yes; contestability is about ease of market entry rather than the size of firms

***examiner's* note** It is common in the UK to measure three- or five-firm concentration ratios, while four firms tend to be the norm in the USA. Concentration ratios are one of several measures used to determine the degree of monopoly power in an industry. The greater the monopoly power, the more chance that producer power will distort markets and create imperfection.

 **24 ANSWERS**

Deadweight loss

Q1 Identify the equilibrium for a monopolist and a competitive firm.

Q2 What is the deadweight loss of an industry being monopolised?

Q3 Explain how a deadweight loss occurs in an industry with externalities.

Q4 Is it possible for a monopolist to produce at lower price and higher output than a competitive industry?

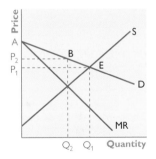

ANSWERS

the differences in utility between a private equilibrium and the social optimum

A1 P_1Q_1 for a competitive industry; P_2Q_2 for a monopolist

A2 P_1AE is the consumer surplus before monopolisation and P_2AB after, therefore the deadweight loss is P_1EBP_2

A3 the equilibrium for the industry is different from the social optimum, producing a deadweight loss

A4 yes, if the monopolist experiences significant economies of scale not available to the competitive firms

***examiner's* note** Based on the assumption of 'given costs', the monopolisation of a competitive industry will produce higher prices and lower output. However, the removal of the given cost assumption and the likelihood of economies of scale can shift the cost curves far enough to produce a lower price and a higher output under monopoly.

Price discrimination

Q1 What is perfect price discrimination?

Q2 What characteristics must be in place for discrimination to succeed?

Q3 Perfect price discrimination eliminates the c............. s.............

Q4 With reference to the diagram, is it possible to price discriminate profitably?

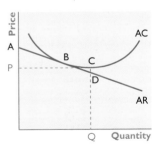

ANSWERS

when a producer charges different prices to different customers for the same product

A1 charging each consumer the maximum price they are willing to pay rather than a single price to all customers

A2 monopoly supply, clear market segmentation and no resale between market segments

A3 *consumer surplus*

A4 as long as the triangle PAB is larger than BCD, a discriminating firm can make a profit even when a single price is loss making

***examiner's* note** Perfect price discrimination occurs when each customer can be separated and charged the price he or she is willing to pay for a product. Markets can also be segmented into a number of groups and, as long as the elasticity of demand varies between the segments, it is profitable to price discriminate. If a firm discriminates perfectly, then the demand curve becomes the marginal revenue curve and the average revenue curve shifts outward.

Monopoly profit

Q1 Can a monopolist control price and output?

Q2 Can monopoly profits be maintained over the long run?

Q3 How has the government tried to deal with the problem of monopoly profits in the newly privatised utilities?

Q4 Identify a way in which monopoly profits could be used beneficially.

ANSWERS

excessive profit earned by the single firm industry and sustained through entry barriers

A1 no; a monopolist can control either price or output but not both

A2 yes; barriers to entry stop competition and protect monopoly profits

A3 it has set up a regulator for each utility and they have a significant degree of control over price and profits

A4 for charitable and good causes, for research and development, or to improve the quality of the product

***examiner's* note** Monopoly profits are usually considered to be an example of a market imperfection that leads to an inefficient allocation of resources. In a competitive situation, these supernormal profits are eroded as new firms are attracted to supply this market and take a share of the excessive profits. Monopoly profits therefore require significant barriers to stop new firms entering the industry. Examples of these barriers are technical economies, patents and unique locations.

Multinational corporation (MNC)

Q1 What is the difference between an MNC and a company that sells its products in many different countries?

Q2 Give three examples of multinational corporations.

Q3 Identify two advantages of being an MNC.

Q4 Why is local knowledge important to MNCs?

ANSWERS

an international company based in one country but with subsidiaries in other countries

A1 to be an MNC it is necessary not only to sell in other countries, but also to produce in them

A2 Shell; BP; Microsoft; Intel; Coca-Cola; Carlsberg

A3 economies of scale; taking advantage of different costs in different countries, e.g. labour, tax breaks, interest rates

A4 in order to maintain good industrial relations and market share it is necessary to understand local culture and customs

***examiner's* note** HSBC, the international bank, uses an advertising campaign that refers to it as the world's local bank. It boasts knowledge of local customs and points out how important it is for international companies to be aware of things that will take their business forward as well as things which, if they get them wrong, will damage production and/or sales of their products.

Public–private partnership

Q1 What is nationalisation?

Q2 What is privatisation?

Q3 Identify three nationalised industries that have been privatised.

Q4 Why have some partial privatisations involved a public–private partnership?

ANSWERS ▶▶

government and private firms joining together to resource a particular economic activity

A1 the transfer of private firms into the public sector, where they trade under state ownership and control

A2 the transfer of state-owned assets into the private sector, usually through a share sale

A3 examples are gas, electricity, water, transport, telecommunications, steel, railways

A4 this usually occurs where only parts of the activity are expected to be profitable and therefore attractive to the private sector

examiner's **note** Initially, nationalisation was the chosen option when certain economic activities were seen as strategically important or likely to produce natural monopolies that had potential to exploit the consumer. Over time, due to the lack of a market discipline, many of these activities were returned to the private sector with some sort of regulatory control to offset potential market imperfections.

(29) ANSWERS

Deregulation

Q1 What is the difference between deregulation and privatisation?

Q2 Are regulations necessary in a market place?

Q3 Why has deregulation become a chosen policy of government?

Q4 Give an example of deregulation not linked to privatisation.

ANSWERS

> the removal of rules, regulations and laws
> which have been judged to impose
> restrictions on competition

A1 privatisation is transferring state assets to the private sector;
    deregulation includes changes in the public or private sector of
    the economy

A2 yes, in order to produce 'a level playing field' for competing
    producers and consumers

A3 it is a recognition of the benefits accruing from competition

A4 removal of restrictions on foreign firms setting up in the UK;
    competitive tendering in the public services; contract work in
    hospitals and schools

examiner's note Since the 1980s there has been a greater recognition
among parties of all political persuasion that the suppression of competition had,
in many industries, produced a variety of inefficiencies, including lack of
motivation, lack of market discipline, an administrative bureaucracy to manage
rules and regulations, and a lack of innovation.

Privatisation

Q1 Give two reasons why private firms are nationalised.

Q2 Identify three nationalised industries that have been privatised.

Q3 Identify two different ways that privatisation can take place.

Q4 What is the concern regarding privatisation and natural monopoly?

ANSWERS ▶▶

the transfer of state-owned industry back to the private sector of the economy

A1 fear of monopoly exploitation; duplication of resources; strategic reasons; job protection

A2 gas; electricity; water; rail network; steel; telephones

A3 sell-off of shares to the public; placement of shares with existing firms; transfer of assets to employees

A4 many nationalised industries had the potential to become natural monopolies through technical economies of scale and this allowed them to raise prices and reduce output

***examiner's* note** The failure of the nationalised industries to perform satisfactorily was due to lack of competition and their endless requirement for funds to support their inefficiency. Privatisation, the development of competition and a regulator were seen as possible solutions to the inefficiency of the nationalised sector. The jury is still out on whether the result is an unmitigated success.

Utility regulator

Q1 What happened to a number of utilities that led to the setting up of a regulator?

Q2 What is a natural monopoly?

Q3 What is meant by RPI − X?

Q4 Why may it no longer be necessary to have a telecommunications regulator?

ANSWERS

A1 public utilities with the potential to become natural monopolies were privatised

A2 when a firm gains control of an industry without that being its intention

A3 retail price index minus an X factor that takes account of the potential for utilities to cut costs and improve efficiency

A4 there is now considerable competition in this industry, which will keep prices down and promote productivity

***examiner's* note** The privatised utilities, such as gas, electricity, telecommunications, transport and water, have a tendency towards natural monopoly caused by their location and significant economies of scale. To counter this, powerful regulators were set up to ensure that the new entrants into the private sector of the economy did not abuse their status and restrict output, raise prices and make excessive profits.

Sustainable transport system

Q1 What is the main cause and effect of carbon dioxide emissions?

Q2 Given current trends, rank the following modes of transport from more sustainable to less sustainable: travelling by foot, car, train or bicycle.

Q3 The government has stated that a sustainable transport system requires an i........... t........... p...........

Q4 What is the most efficient mechanism for reallocating resources among the transport modes?

ANSWERS

where supplying current transport needs does not compromise the supply required to meet future needs

A1 car exhausts are the main cause; global warming is arguably the main effect

A2 foot, bicycle, train, car (given the rate at which they use up resources)

A3 *integrated transport policy*

A4 the price mechanism is the best way of encouraging and discouraging use

***examiner's* note** In a mixed economy the best way to reallocate resources is through the price mechanism. For example, the easiest way to encourage the use of unleaded petrol was to reduce the tax on that type of petrol while setting a relatively higher tax on leaded petrol. There are now very few users of leaded petrol and the relative price of each type of petrol has been equalised as oil companies seek to make more profit from the unleaded version.

Transport modes

Q1 Identify three different transport modes.

Q2 Which domestic transport mode is the most flexible and convenient?

Q3 Which form of freight transport, if available, is cheapest per unit of weight over long distances?

Q4 Except for joy riding, transport is a d_____ demand.

ANSWERS

the different ways in which people and products are moved from place to place

A1 roads; railways; sea; waterways; air; pipelines

A2 cars and roads offer the opportunity to achieve a door-to-door service

A3 inland and international waterways

A4 *derived* — the demand for transport is derived from the demand for products in final demand

***examiner's* note** Traditionally, transport modes are concerned with the movement of people and freight using road, rail, inland and international waterways, air and pipelines. Communication channels are mainly used to move ideas from place to place, but they can also be used to transport products, e.g. downloading computer programmes across the internet. The cheapest forms of transport by weight are usually the most expensive in terms of time and vice versa.

Congestion cost

Q1 What is meant by traffic congestion?

Q2 Identify two external costs of traffic congestion.

Q3 To be successful, road pricing must take account of
p............ e............ of d............

Q4 Identify two options, other than road pricing, that can be
used to tackle congestion.

ANSWERS

A1 an abnormal accumulation of traffic which causes delays

A2 exhaust pollution; lost time; road rage; stress

A3 *price elasticity; demand* — this is important if enough traffic is to be discouraged from using the road

A4 petrol taxes; increase road space; restrict road use; restrict road users (e.g. by increasing driving licence age)

***examiner's* note** Congestion on the roads has become an increasing problem over recent years, despite attempts to raise the cost of travel and the introduction of congestion charges. The congestion charge in London seems to have caused a redistribution of congestion rather than an overall reduction: the roads just outside the charging area have seen a considerable increase in traffic as cars search for alternative routes without charges.

(35) **ANSWERS**

Road pricing

Q1 Give an example of a positive externality from building a motorway to the west country.

Q2 Are roads private or public goods?

Q3 Which negative externality is road pricing trying to tackle?

Q4 Give an example of road pricing in the UK.

ANSWERS

a price paid by road users directly related to the stretch of road used at a particular time

A1 an increase in the number of tourists visiting the west country

A2 some roads are non-rival and non-excludable and therefore public goods; others, e.g. motorways with tolls, can be made rival and excludable

A3 congestion

A4 congestion charge in London or toll roads and bridges

examiner's **note** Technology has made it possible to consider road pricing in areas where the roads were originally non-rival and non-excludable. Cameras and computers can be set up to record who uses roads and charge accordingly. It may also be possible, in the future, to establish a bar coding system that identifies which cars are using which roads for how long and charge the car owner. At present, the indirect way of charging for road use is to impose a tax on petrol such that the more petrol used, the more tax paid.

Integrated transport policy

Q1 The 1997 consultative document 'developing an Integrated Transport Policy' stated that the f............. g............. in r............. t............. is unacceptable.

Q2 Do cars produce more positive or negative externalities?

Q3 Identify a positive externality caused by rail travel.

Q4 Which negative externality is a road-building programme likely to reduce?

ANSWERS

designed to create fewer externalities and more efficiency in the use of different means of transport

A1 *forecast growth; road traffic*

A2 cars produce more negative externalities in the form of congestion and pollution

A3 a reduction in congestion and pollution from cars

A4 as it increases the availability of roads, it is likely to reduce congestion

***examiner's* note** In the past, transport policies have often targeted each of the modes of transport individually, without consideration of other ways of moving people and freight around the country. By 1997 it was realised that the only way to raise efficiency across all transport modes was to integrate policies and consider the overall impact, on all forms of transport, of individual decisions in each transport sector. For example, to raise the price of road travel would reduce negative externalities and encourage more rail travel.

 **(37) ANSWERS**

Labour mobility

Q1 Distinguish between the two generally recognised types of labour mobility.

Q2 What is the relationship between labour mobility and economic growth?

Q3 Identify two ways in which labour mobility may be increased.

Q4 There are always f............ that hold back labour mobility.

ANSWERS

A1 geographical (lateral) and occupational (vertical) mobility

A2 the faster the rate of economic growth, the greater the need for labour to be more mobile

A3 education and training; grants and subsidies; differential rewards

A4 *frictions*

***examiner's* note** It is not necessary for all labour to be mobile, although the faster the rate of economic growth the more mobility is required to satisfy the changing conditions of supply and demand. Within any labour force there are more and less mobile groups. The less mobile groups may be held back by age, infirmity, inability to develop new skills, sunk costs, family commitments and medical conditions such as the stress associated with new jobs and new locations.

Marginal physical product

Q1 Over what range is there increasing and diminishing marginal returns?

Q2 What causes increasing marginal returns in the short run?

Q3 Define the law of variable proportions.

Q4 What causes diminishing marginal returns in the short run?

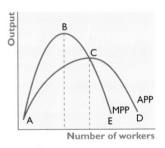

ANSWERS

the addition to total output when one more factor of production is employed

A1 AB = increasing marginal returns; BE = diminishing marginal returns

A2 adding the variable factor labour allows the firm to take advantage of division of labour and specialisation of function

A3 at some point, while adding variable factors to a fixed factor, the additions to output will begin to diminish

A4 often the fixed factor is limited space and adding more productive factors eventually causes problems

***examiner's* note** Quite often the saying 'too many cooks spoil the broth' is used to indicate the problems of working in confined spaces. It is important to note that the law of variable proportions is about output (returns) and not costs, although it does have implications for costs. If a firm continues to spend equal amounts on employing variable factors and the additions to output are diminishing, then at some point marginal and average costs will start to rise.

Marginal revenue productivity

Q1 How much labour will be employed at W_1?

Q2 How much labour will be employed at W_3?

Q3 Where is the demand curve for labour?

Q4 Under what circumstance would an employer choose W_2Q_4 as an equilibrium?

ANSWERS

A1 the profit-maximising equilibrium is W_1Q_3, where the marginal cost of labour equals the marginal revenue product (MRP)

A2 no one will be employed as it is not profitable to employ anyone when the wage rises above the highest point on the average revenue product curve (ARP)

A3 MRP below ARP

A4 if the employer wanted to return the total revenue received from employing Q_4 of labour to the workforce

***examiner's* note** MRP below ARP is the demand curve for labour: assuming that the firm is profit maximising, there is only one variable factor of production, the demand for the product is perfectly elastic and the supply of the productive factor is perfectly elastic. If any of these assumptions does not apply, then the above described rule changes.

Equilibrium wage rate

Q1 What assumptions are made about competition in the market illustrated?

Q2 What will happen if the wage rate is at W_2?

Q3 Describe the shift and movement that would produce an equilibrium at W_2Q_2.

Q4 Could a trade union maintain employment at W_1Q?

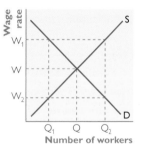

ANSWERS

WQ is the point at which labour supplied to the market is equal to the quantity demanded

A1 there must be people competing for the job and employers competing to hire them

A2 the quantity demanded will exceed the quantity supplied and employers will bid up wages to attract more labour

A3 the supply curve would have to shift to the right moving down the demand curve

A4 yes, if it threatens disruptive actions and the employers agree to transfer potential profits to the wage bill rather than suffer the costs of a strike

***examiner's* note** The theory of wages illustrated above is a static equilibrium model that assumes unrealistic levels of knowledge, competition and mobility. In reality, labour markets are dynamic, knowledge is imperfect and frictions hold back mobility.

 ANSWERS

Supply of labour curve

Q1 Will a higher wage rate shift the curve to the left or right?

Q2 What is the difference between a shift and a movement?

Q3 Identify one factor that will shift S to S_2.

Q4 Identify one factor that will shift S to S_1.

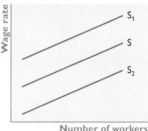

Number of workers

ANSWERS

shows the relationship between wages and the number of people willing to work in a particular labour market

A1 it will not shift the curve; it produces a movement along the curve

A2 a shift is more or less supply at the same wage; a movement is more or less supply at a different wage

A3 lower relative wage rates or decline in other labour markets from which skills are transferable

A4 higher relative wage rates or expansion in other labour markets

***examiner's* note** Supply curves vary from one labour market to another as a result of the fact that labour is not homogeneous. Because some people are taller, stronger, more able intellectually, more motivated, have better sight, better eye/limb coordination, bigger lung capacity etc. there are many different labour markets between which skills are not perfectly transferable. Some skills can be learnt; others are gifts at birth.

 ANSWERS

Supply of effort curve

Q1 The shape of the curve depends on the trade-off between w............... and l...............

Q2 Explain the shape of the curve between A and B.

Q3 Explain the shape of the curve between B and C.

Q4 What is the difference between this curve and a market supply of labour curve?

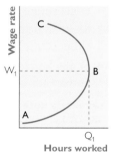

shows the relationship between wage rates
and the number of hours per day a person
is willing to work

A1 *work; leisure*

A2 between A and B a higher wage rate encourages the person
to substitute work for leisure

A3 between B and C a higher wage rate encourages the person
to substitute leisure for work

A4 on the horizontal axis the market supply curve shows number
of workers, not hours worked

***examiner's* note** In the diagram, as the wage rate increases to W_1 a worker
is attracted to work more hours because marginal leisure hours are less valuable.
After W_1 the marginal leisure hours become more valuable and the worker
chooses to work fewer hours for a similar total wage rather than more hours for
a higher total wage. This curve should not be confused with the supply of labour
curve to a given labour market, which shows the number of people willing to
work in that labour market.

(43) **ANSWERS**

Labour market elasticity

Q1 Identify one factor that will produce a relatively inelastic demand for labour.

Q2 Relate substitution to elasticity of supply.

Q3 Will a relatively inelastic supply of labour always produce a relatively high wage rate?

Q4 Relate economic rent to elasticity of supply.

ANSWERS))

the responsiveness of demand or supply of labour to a change in the wage rate

A1 a relatively inelastic demand for the product or a capital intensive industry where labour costs are a small fraction of total costs

A2 relatively easy substitution of one unit of labour for another will produce a more elastic supply curve and vice versa

A3 no, it depends on the position of the demand curve for labour

A4 economic rent is a greater proportion of the reward to labour the more inelastic the supply curve

***examiner's* note** It is a common mistake to assume that high or low wages depend on either a relatively inelastic supply or demand for labour. Examination candidates often say that high educational qualifications will automatically produce high incomes. This is not the case as it is the interaction of supply and demand which is the main influence on the equilibrium wage. This means that some graduates will achieve high incomes but other equally competent graduates will end up with low incomes.

 ANSWERS

Economic rent

Q1 The term comes from rent as a s............... reward to l...............

Q2 Why are premier league footballers likely to earn economic rent?

Q3 Identify the area of economic rent on the diagram.

Q4 Under what circumstances would a factor receive only economic rent?

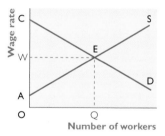

A1 *surplus; land*

A2 the next best income they can earn is likely to be a lot less than they earn as a professional footballer

A3 WEA is the area above transfer earning OAEQ

A4 if the supply curve was perfectly inelastic

examiner's **note** Because there was no cost of producing land, the owners of land were considered to be receiving a reward that was a surplus. This idea was developed further when the term economic rent was applied to any reward to a productive factor over and above the minimum required to keep that factor in a particular line of business. In the case of the entrepreneur, excessive profit is an economic rent, whereas normal profit is a transfer earning.

Transfer earning

Q1 Which area represents the transfer earning?

Q2 Which unit of labour only receives a transfer earning?

Q3 If a person could earn £25,000 and is earning £35,000, what is the transfer earning?

Q4 What is the equivalent transfer earning for an entrepreneur?

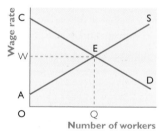

ANSWERS

the minimum reward required to keep a factor of production in its current use

A1 OAEQ

A2 the last unit of labour employed at Q receives a wage equal to the transfer earning

A3 £25,000 is the transfer earning

A4 normal profit is the minimum amount required to keep an entrepreneur in a particular line of business

***examiner's* note** The transfer earning is not always the same as the wage rate. In the diagram on this card the supply curve would have to be perfectly elastic for the wage rate to equal the transfer earning. Normally, most wage rates comprise two elements, including the transfer earning and the economic rent. Ideally, employers would like to know the split so they could increase profits by reducing wages to the minimum required to keep each employee in the current job. Fortunately for employees, this information is unavailable.

 **ANSWERS**

Monopsony buyer of labour

Q1 Why is there a divergence between MC and S?

Q2 Where is the equilibrium for a monopsonist?

Q3 What happens to employment if a trade union is able to raise the wage from W_3 to W_2?

Q4 If the trade union raised the wage above W_2, what would happen?

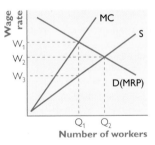

ANSWERS

a sole buyer of all of the labour in one labour market

A1 each time the monopsonist wants to buy more labour, the wage rate has to be raised for all the workers

A2 W_3Q_1 is where MC equals MRP

A3 employment will increase from Q_1 to Q_2

A4 employment would be reduced

***examiner's* note** A common mistake is to identify W_1Q_1 as the monopsony equilibrium where the equality between MC and MRP occurs at a wage rate of W_3. A second difficulty is to realise that when a trade union enters this particular labour market there is a range over which it can raise wages and it becomes profitable to employ more people. This is because the agreed trade union influenced wage provides a floor below which wages cannot fall, although they can always rise above that floor.

 **ANSWERS**

National minimum wage (NMW)

Q1 The NMW is concerned with the problem of l............ p............ and p............

Q2 From the diagram identify the effect of an NMW set at W_1.

Q3 What effect will an NMW set at W_2 have on the labour market?

Q4 When can a rise in the NMW be a fall in wages?

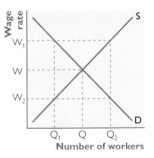

ANSWERS

a floor below which wages cannot legally fall

A1 *low pay; poverty*

A2 demand for labour will fall from Q to Q_1 while those people willing to work will rise from Q to Q_2, producing an unemployed surplus of $Q_2 - Q_1$

A3 it will have no effect on the market equilibrium WQ as it is below the market rate

A4 if the rate of inflation is greater than the nominal rise in the NMW

***examiner's* note** In some countries, the minimum wage has been established with reference to an hourly rate, while others have set a minimum rate for an agreed working week. The UK government has set a lowest level of payment for an hourly rate that applies to all workers over the age of 21. This is an interesting area of analysis because the NMW will only be effective if it is above the rate currently being paid in some labour markets. The resultant distortion will be an involuntary group of unemployed people.

Collective bargaining

Q1 Under which circumstances is a trade union a monopoly supplier of labour?

Q2 If a trade union aims to raise wage rates, is it more likely to shift the supply or demand curve for labour?

Q3 A firm may agree to raise wages after estimating the cost of the proposed i............ a............

Q4 Identify two reasons why employment may not fall after an agreed wage increase.

ANSWERS

negotiations, usually by a trade union, with an employer on behalf of all the employees

A1 if the trade union is a closed shop so that only members of the union can gain employment

A2 usually the supply curve is shifted to the left if a trade union becomes involved in restricting the supply of labour

A3 *industrial action* — this can be a significant cost to a firm

A4 demand for the product is perfectly inelastic or shifting to the right; labour productivity has increased; a monopsony buyer of labour exists in the market

***examiner's* note** The alternative to collective bargaining is each employee bargaining individually with an employer. As a group, employees are more powerful, particularly when they can threaten strike action and disrupt production plans. Over recent years the power of the trade union has been weakened by legislation which prevents secondary picketing, imposes limitations on the closed shop and requires secret ballots.

49 ANSWERS

Equal Pay Act (EPA)

Q1 Which two groups of people is the EPA focused on?

Q2 The fundamental aim of the act was to remove d............. in the labour market.

Q3 Recently it was claimed that, after 30 years, women still earn less than 80% of the male wage rate in similar jobs. Does this mean the act has failed?

Q4 Positive discrimination (PD) has been suggested as a way of increasing the number of women in top jobs. What is PD?

ANSWERS ▶▶

introduced in 1970, it states that employers are required to give equal payment to men and women

A1 men and women

A2 *discrimination*

A3 yes, if it is still the result of discrimination; no, if there are relevant economic explanations

A4 reserving a number of top jobs for women only

***examiner's* note** The law applies where men and women are employed on the same or broadly similar work or, if the work is different, then the woman's job must be rated as equivalent to that of a man by means of a job evaluation exercise. The differences in male and female wage rates and the lack of women in top jobs may be explained by some women being less motivated, having different lifetime goals and having career breaks to bring up children.

Circular flow of income

Q1 Identify three injections to and three withdrawals from the circular flow.

Q2 Complete the general equilibrium equation:
Y = ...

Q3 What is the difference between autonomous and induced investment?

Q4 What effect would an increasing deficit on the current account of the balance of payments have on the circular flow of income?

ANSWERS

money flow that passes through the economy in the opposite direction to the flow of products and assets

A1 injections include investment, government expenditure and exports; withdrawals include saving, taxation and imports

A2 national income (Y) = consumption (C) + investment (I) + government expenditure (G) + exports (E) − imports (M)

A3 autonomous investment is unrelated to changes in national income; induced investment results directly from an increase in national income

A4 there would be a net withdrawal from the flow as X < M

***examiner's* note** A common mistake is to assume that consumption is an injection into the circular flow of income. This assumption is incorrect because consumption is always measured inside the flow. Although three main withdrawals and three main injections are used in models of the circular flow, in practice there are other relevant withdrawals and injections, e.g. if people hoard cash rather than save in a recognised institution, money is withdrawn rather than recycled through the economy.

(51) **ANSWERS**

Components of aggregate demand

Q1 Is consumption an injection to or a withdrawal from the circular flow of income?

Q2 Differentiate between induced and autonomous investment.

Q3 Induced investment has an a................... effect on the economy, while autonomous investment has a m................... effect.

Q4 Is it possible for all the components of aggregate demand to increase and for GDP to fall?

ANSWERS

consumption (C) + investment (I) + government expenditure (G) + exports (X) – imports (M)

A1 it is neither as it is internal to the circular flow model

A2 induced investment results from a change in GDP; autonomous investment changes GDP

A3 *accelerator; multiplier*

A4 yes, if the rate of nominal change in the components increases through inflation while real output declines

***examiner's* note** A further component of aggregate demand which is sometimes included in descriptions is stock building. This is, in effect, producers buying their own products so that they can accommodate fluctuations in demand which may be expected (seasonal) or unexpected (shock). An aggregate demand shock is a sudden and unexpected change in any of the components of aggregate demand. Shocks may have significant real effects on the economy that could be beneficial or damaging.

Marginal propensity to consume (MPC)

Q1 What does an MPC of 0.75 mean?

Q2 If the average propensity to consume is rising, what is happening to the MPC?

Q3 What do Keynesians say will happen to the MPC as incomes rise?

Q4 Will the multiplier effect on income increase or decrease if the MPC increases?

ANSWERS

the proportion of additional income received that is spent on consumer products

A1 for each additional £1 received, 75p will be spent on consumption

A2 if the average number is rising, the marginal number must also be rising

A3 they predict that the MPC will begin to fall at some point as income rises

A4 if MPC increases, there are less withdrawals from the flow of income, so the multiplier effect will increase

***examiner's* note** There are three main theories of what happens to the MPC as income rises. The Keynesian approach assumes a point where the MPC falls as income rises. Milton Friedman suggests a permanent income hypothesis, which states that current income is less important than a perception of permanent income in determining consumption. Franco Modigliani and others identified a life cycle hypothesis, which suggests that the effect of a change in income on consumption depends upon the life stage of the recipient.

Multiplier

Q1 What is the balanced budget multiplier?

Q2 Complete the formula for the multiplier in an open economy with a government: K = ...

Q3 If MPM = 0.2, MPS = 0.1 and MPT = 0.1, what is the value of the multiplier?

Q4 If an economy is made up of two groups of consumers with MPCs of 0.8 and 0.9, what can you say about an injection of £25m into the economy?

ANSWERS

the number of times an injection into
or withdrawal from the economy changes
total income

A1 it always has the value of 1 such that an increase in expenditure
and taxation of £10m raises income by £10m

A2 $K = \dfrac{1}{MPM + MPS + MPT}$ or $K = \dfrac{1}{MPW}$

A3 $\dfrac{1}{0.4}$ = a multiplier of 2.5

A4 the multipliers will be 5 and 10 for the two groups respectively,
so income will rise between £125m and £250m

***examiner's* note** The multiplier is a Keynesian concept that assumes fixed
prices and therefore a change in real income as the result of injections into or
withdrawals from the circular flow of income. Other interpretations of the multiplier
which accept variable prices predict that the total change in income as a result of
an injection or withdrawal may be real (a growth in output), nominal (an inflation or
deflation) or shared between a change in prices and a change in output.

Accelerator theory

Q1 What is the capital/output ratio?

Q2 Complete the equation for the accelerator:
I = ...

Q3 What is the difference between the accelerator and the multiplier?

Q4 If capital is valued at 100 and 10% of capital consumed is replaced each year, what will happen if real GDP grows by 50% in 1 year?

ANSWERS

a theory of the relationship between a change in national income and its effect on investment

A1 the numerical relationship between the amount of capital required and the total output of the economy

A2 $I = f(\Delta Y)$, i.e. investment is a function of a change in national income

A3 the accelerator is the induced effect on investment of a change in national income; the multiplier is the effect of an autonomous change in investment

A4 in the first year investment in capital will rise from 10 to 60 units (50 new investment and 10 replacement) before settling to 15 replacement units in successive years

***examiner's* note** The accelerator theory is part of a Keynesian analysis of economic instability and can work over time with the multiplier to generate cyclical activity. An autonomous increase in investment will cause a multiple increase in real GDP.

(55) **ANSWERS**

Inflationary/deflationary gap

Q1 What is W, and why is it upward sloping?

Q2 What is J, and why is it horizontal?

Q3 Given Y_e and Y_{f1}, what is CD?

Q4 Given Y_e and Y_f, what is AB?

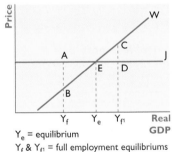

Y_e = equilibrium
Y_f & Y_{f1} = full employment equilibriums

ANSWERS

A1 W represents withdrawals, which increase as real GDP rises

A2 J represents injections, which do not change as real GDP rises

A3 CD is a deflationary gap

A4 AB is an inflationary gap

***examiner's* note** These are Keynesian concepts that assume full employment
and less than or more than full employment equilibriums. W is related to changes
in real GDP in as much as a rise in real GDP will increase tax revenue,
expenditure on imports and savings. However, J is assumed to be autonomous in
as much as investment, government expenditure and demand for imports are
assumed to be unrelated to changes in real GDP. The gaps can be closed by
shifts in either W or J, or both.

Full employment

Q1 Explain the terms 'under-full employment' and 'over-full employment'.

Q2 Identify four different types of unemployment.

Q3 At full employment, will the economy be producing at its full productive potential?

Q4 In the Keynesian model of full employment, which two policies are used to fine-tune the economy?

ANSWERS

Keynesian model of employment where there are sufficient jobs available for all who seek work

A1 under-full employment is a level of unemployment which can be reduced by expanding aggregate demand; over-full employment is a level of employment which will lead to inflation if aggregate demand increases

A2 casual; cyclical; structural; frictional; seasonal; disguised

A3 ideally yes, but in practice no, as there will always be people in the process of moving jobs, i.e. frictional unemployment

A4 monetary and fiscal policy are used as demand-management policies

***examiner's* note** The government stopped referring to full employment as an achievable target after a number of unsuccessful attempts during the 1970s and 1980s to manipulate demand to achieve a higher level of employment. Unemployment has now fallen to a sustainable low, arguably as the result of supply-side policies designed to create more flexible labour markets.

Consumer price index (CPI)

Q1 To what is the CPI of the Bank of England equivalent?

Q2 Both the European Central Bank (ECB) and Bank of England have an inflation target of 2%. What is the difference between them?

Q3 What is the main difference in the composition of the RPI and the CPI?

Q4 There is a significant difference in the formulas used to calculate the RPI and CPI. What is it?

ANSWERS ▶▶

the new calculation used to measure inflation in the UK

A1 the harmonised index of consumer prices (HICP) of the European Central Bank

A2 the ECB target is less than 2%; the Bank of England is +/–1% of a 2% target

A3 the RPI included many housing costs, which are excluded in the CPI

A4 the formula used to calculate RPI is arithmetic, whereas the CPI formula is geometric

***examiner's* note** The CPI usually produces a measured lower rate of inflation than RPI. One of the main reasons for this is the difference between arithmetic and geometric calculations. For example, if two products each cost £4: an arithmetic average is $4 + 4 = 8 \div 2 = 4$; a geometric calculation is $\sqrt{4 \times 4} = 4$. Double the price of one product and halve the other: arithmetic $= 8 + 2 = 10 \div 2 = 5$, a rise of 20%; geometric $\sqrt{8 \times 2} = 4$, which gives no change in average prices.

Augmented Phillips curve

Q1 What was the original function that A.W. Phillips identified?

Q2 Between which two variables did the original Phillips curve produce a trade-off?

Q3 Why did the 1970s raise a question mark over the predictive ability of the Phillips curve?

Q4 What is NAIRU?

ANSWERS ⟫

incorporates a price variable into the original Phillips curve

A1 his original research showed a relationship between the level of employment and wages such that low unemployment initiated higher wages and vice versa

A2 inflation and employment levels, such that higher levels of employment could be achieved with more inflation

A3 inflation and unemployment rose together; this is not predicted by the Phillips curve

A4 non-accelerating inflation rate of unemployment (often referred to imprecisely as the natural level of unemployment); it suggests a long-run vertical Phillips curve

***examiner's* note** The augmented Phillips curve is also referred to as the expectations-adjusted curve.

Cyclical instability

Q1 Which terms are used to describe events in one cycle of economic activity?

Q2 Identify two causes of cyclical instability.

Q3 Which policy and what limits are imposed to deal with cyclical instability in the EU?

Q4 What do monetarists suggest is the solution to cyclical instability?

ANSWERS

repetitive cycle of economic events, e.g. the business cycle, the trade cycle

A1 the most common are boom, recession, depression and recovery

A2 economic events that produce excessive demand and initiate a boom, or that produce excessive supply and initiate a slump

A3 the 'Stability and Growth Pact' imposes a 3% limit on budget deficits and limits national debt to 60% of GDP

A4 steady and stable growth in money supply in line with the growth in output of the economy

***examiner's* note** There is much debate among economists about whether cyclical instability is an inevitable by-product of a capitalist society that needs to be controlled as it cannot be cured, or whether cyclical instability is fundamentally a problem caused by incompetent management of the economy, particularly in the use of monetary and fiscal policy. In the second case, the cure is in the hands of politicians and their appointed representatives.

Costs of economic growth

Q1 What is the opportunity cost of economic growth?

Q2 If an economy fails to grow, is it possible for people's real income to rise?

Q3 What external costs of consumption are likely to occur as real incomes rise?

Q4 What are the personal costs to individuals of faster rates of economic growth?

ANSWERS ▶▶

damaging economic effects of a growth in per capita productive capacity

A1 for an economy to grow, current consumption must be foregone

A2 yes, but only as part of a redistributive process where some people become better off as others become worse off

A3 rising car ownership increases the problems of congestion and pollution

A4 faster rates require increased labour mobility which can increase stress and cause nervous breakdowns

***examiner's* note** When answering questions on the costs and benefits of economic growth, it is useful to remember the following three costs: opportunity cost (most commonly missed out in answers); personal costs caused by the requirement to become more occupationally and geographically mobile; and the external costs to society of both the increased production and consumption of goods and services.

 ANSWERS

Limits to economic growth

Q1 What is the main benefit of economic growth?

Q2 What are non-renewable resources?

Q3 What is the doomsday prediction which takes account of population growth and non-renewable resources?

Q4 What are the two opposing solutions to the threat of a growth-induced doomsday?

ANSWERS ▶▶

problems that slow economic growth and eventually bring about economic stagnation and decline

A1 it can raise standards of living for all or some people without lowering living standards for others

A2 they include natural resources like coal, gas and oil that cannot be replaced once they have been used

A3 population growth is accelerating and will soon use up all the non-renewable resources and standards of living will suddenly fall

A4 one is to allow market forces and the price mechanism to work; the other is a government-managed rationing of resources

***examiner's* note** The doomsday scenario postulates that the world will drift into conflict and war over a dwindling amount of natural resources. The alternative view of market economists is that as resources become more scarce so prices will rise, and it will become more profitable to utilise other resources and search for synthetic substitutes.

Sustainable economic growth

Q1 Is it possible for economic growth not to be sustainable?

Q2 Use of which resources puts sustainability at risk?

Q3 Name two current events that have raised concern about the potential damage of unsustainable economic growth.

Q4 As resources become more scarce, which mechanism can be used to allocate increasingly scarce resources to where they are most in demand?

ANSWERS

> to be sustainable, economic growth
> must produce benefits that can be
> replicated again and again

A1 yes, if the benefits cannot be replicated

A2 non-renewable resources

A3 possible answers include: deforestation; over-fishing; global
warming; pollution of various types

A4 the price mechanism

***examiner's* note** There is significant controversy over whether the use of
non-renewable resources, e.g. coal, gas and oil, needs to be managed into the
future to make growth more sustainable; or whether the market mechanism
provides a process that will slow down consumption as the price rises and make
it more profitable to search for alternative ways of providing the benefits
currently received from non-renewable resources.

 63 ANSWERS

Absolute poverty

Q1 What is the difference between absolute and relative poverty?

Q2 Does poverty exist in more economically developed countries?

Q3 What is the poverty trap?

Q4 Identify a short-term and a long-term solution to poverty.

ANSWERS

when a person does not have access to sufficient resources to sustain a healthy life

A1 poverty is identified in more economically developed countries at a much higher standard of living than in less economically developed countries, which are closer to absolute poverty

A2 relative poverty exists as measured by an agreed poverty line

A3 poor people lose entitlement to benefits as their income rises but still pay tax on their marginal income

A4 short-term solutions usually involve redistributive policies; long-term solutions are linked to economic growth

***examiner's* note** A significant proportion of the world's population lives below the poverty lines drawn for the more developed world and is below or close to absolute poverty. Famines, malnutrition, the ravages of war, high death rates, low life expectancy and endemic diseases are all characteristics of poverty.

 **ANSWERS**

Negative income tax

Q1 What are 'negative' and 'regressive' income tax?

Q2 The poverty trap occurs as a result of an overlap between which two variables?

Q3 Negative income tax would go a long way to replacing the current b.................... s....................

Q4 If people start paying income tax when they have earned £5,000, how much will they receive if they earn nothing and negative income tax is 40%?

ANSWERS

payment of a tax credit for every pound not earned below the tax threshold

A1 negative income tax is a credit received by people with low or no incomes; regressive income tax is a falling proportion of rising income paid in tax

A2 tax starts to be paid at a level where some people are still receiving benefits

A3 *benefits system*

A4 40% of £5,000 = £2,000

***examiner's* note** A unified system of tax and negative income tax would remove the poverty trap, in which attempts by low-income earners to increase their earnings cause them to lose entitlement to benefits and to pay tax. Negative income tax would help the poor in the most direct way and leave them the freedom to decide how they spend their money. It would also help to eliminate what some economists judge is a cumbersome and wasteful welfare system.

(65) ANSWERS

Balanced budget

Q1 Can unbalanced budgeting be balanced over time?

Q2 Is it possible to expand or contract the economy by moving from one balanced budget to another balanced budget?

Q3 Is the history of the last 50 years one of balanced or unbalanced budgets?

Q4 Which theoretical model of the economy requires unbalanced budgets?

ANSWERS

when over 1 year the revenue received by government is equal to its expenditure

A1 yes, over several years it is possible for deficits to cancel out surpluses and for a series of budgets to balance

A2 yes, the balanced budget multiplier has a value of one, which means that the economy will expand or contract by one times the rise or fall in expenditure and taxation

A3 unbalanced; almost all the budgets in the last 50 years have been deficits — expenditure has exceeded taxation

A4 Keynesian economics requires deficits and surpluses to fine-tune the economy and reduce the amplitude of cyclical events

***examiner's* note** Many non-Keynesian economists argue that governments should be forced by legislation to balance their budgets every year, or at least over a period of a few years. They argue that governments will always be tempted to overspend their budgets and expand the public sector at the expense of the private sector.

Direct taxation

Q1 Identify three forms of direct taxation.

Q2 On whom does the incidence of tax fall, given direct taxes?

Q3 Why have revenues from inheritance tax increased considerably over recent years?

Q4 Why does the Inland Revenue prefer PAYE taxation to self-employment taxation?

ANSWERS

payment to the Inland Revenue from the income or wealth of individuals or the profits of firms

A1 income tax; corporation tax; inheritance tax; capital gains tax

A2 the receiver of the income

A3 there has been a considerable increase in the value of assets, mainly property, and no corresponding increase in tax thresholds

A4 it is difficult to evade 'pay as you earn' taxation, whereas self-employed people receive income gross and may be tempted not to declare all their earnings

***examiner's* note** Economists analyse taxes with reference to their effect on efficiency, i.e. whether a tax produces a more or less efficient allocation of resources. Questions of fairness, equity and justice are not paramount. An economist may be asked to analyse the likely impact of a range of taxes that will all bring about a less efficient allocation of resources but a more equitable distribution of income and wealth. In this case, the economist is looking for the least effect on efficiency.

Indirect taxation

Q1 Identify two forms of indirect tax.

Q2 On whom does the incidence of tax fall, given indirect taxes?

Q3 Give two circumstances under which the incidence of tax is not shared.

Q4 Explain the statement 'raising indirect taxes can both cause and cure inflation'.

ANSWERS ▶▶

payment to government that is levied on specified products, also known as expenditure taxation

A1 VAT; excise duties; tariffs

A2 it is usually shared between producer and consumer

A3 if price elasticity of demand is perfectly inelastic, the incidence falls entirely on the consumer; if price elasticity of demand is perfectly elastic, it falls on the producer

A4 the immediate effect of raising indirect tax is to raise prices, but the long-term effect is counter-inflationary and will reduce aggregate demand

***examiner's* note** There is considerable debate about whether changes should be made to direct or indirect taxation. The problem with indirect taxation is that the proportion of income paid in tax decreases as income rises. It is therefore easier to manage a government's redistributive policy if it targets direct taxation. However, votes seem to be more forthcoming if income rather than expenditure taxes are reduced.

Public sector borrowing

Q1 Which type of fiscal policy is likely to increase public sector borrowing?

Q2 Which acronyms are commonly used to identify public sector borrowing?

Q3 What is the relationship between public sector borrowing and the real size of the national debt?

Q4 Which type of borrowing is likely to expand the money supply?

ANSWERS

A1 a budget deficit

A2 PSNCR (public sector net cash requirement); PSBR (public sector borrowing requirement)

A3 a yearly borrowing requirement adds to the nominal size of the national debt, while the real size needs to be adjusted for inflation

A4 borrowing that leaves debt unsold at the Bank of England or is financed by selling very liquid assets such as Treasury bills

***examiner's* note** Fiscal and monetary policy are often discussed independently of each other, but they are linked to a significant degree by public sector borrowing. If the government decided to try to expand aggregate demand by budgeting for a deficit, the financing of the borrowing requirement might require a rise in interest rates or an expansion of the money supply, both of which are components of monetary policy.

(69) ANSWERS

Fiscal drag

Q1 Explain progressive income tax using marginal and average tax rates.

Q2 Does fiscal drag act as a built-in stabiliser?

Q3 How can fiscal drag be eliminated from a progressive system of income tax?

Q4 Is fiscal drag cyclical or counter-cyclical?

ANSWERS

the tendency for tax revenues to increase as inflation erodes the value of allowances

A1 if the marginal tax rate exceeds the average tax rate, the tax is progressive

A2 yes, because in an expanding economy an increase in tax acts as a withdrawal from the circular flow

A3 if the income tax bands are index-linked to inflation, then revenue will not increase as the result of nominal changes

A4 it is counter-cyclical as it reduces the amplitude of cyclical fluctuations

***examiner's* note** Some people argue that fiscal drag is an unconstitutional tax because it increases as the result of inflation, not because parliament has decided to increase tax revenue. The counter-cyclical effect of fiscal drag helps suppress inflation during periods when excessive demand is not having the effect of expanding the real output of the economy.

(70) **ANSWERS**

Monetary Policy Committee (MPC)

Q1 What is the structure of the MPC in terms of its membership?

Q2 What is the main target of the MPC?

Q3 What is the main instrument the MPC uses to achieve its target?

Q4 What is the relationship between time lags, interest rates and economic activity?

ANSWERS ▶▶

established along with the Bank of England Act (1998) to manage monetary policy

A1 a governor, two deputy governors, two executive directors from the Bank, and four external members approved by the chancellor

A2 to achieve price stability by maintaining the consumer price index (CPI) at a yearly increase of 2%, +/−1%

A3 raising interest rates (repo rate) to dampen demand and vice versa

A4 a change in interest rates has a time lag of about 15 months for its impact on demand to be fully effective and over 2 years for its full effect on economic activity to be realised

***examiner's* note** The Bank of England has its own model of how interest rate changes are transmitted through the economy. It estimates that a 1% rise in interest rates will cause a fall in demand of between 0.2% and 0.35% and a similar fall in the projected rate of inflation.

 ANSWERS

Five economic tests

Q1 What are the five economic tests?

Q2 What is the problem associated with different countries being at different points in the economic cycle?

Q3 Which macroeconomic policy is no longer available to members once they join the eurozone?

Q4 Which demand management policy is still available to members of the eurozone?

ANSWERS

used to decide whether there is an
unambiguous economic case for
UK membership of the eurozone

A1 compatible business cycles; the flexibility to deal with economic
problems; improvement in long-term investment decisions;
beneficial impact on UK financial services; good for jobs and
growth

A2 one country may require an expansionary policy while another
requires a contractionary policy

A3 monetary policy

A4 fiscal policy

examiner's **note** The British government has stated that a single currency
within a single European market would, in principle, be of benefit to Europe and
the UK and that although constitutional issues need to be taken into account, they
are not overriding. The basis for deciding whether there is an unambiguous case
for joining the eurozone is whether the UK passes the five economic tests. If this
happens, a national referendum will decide on replacing sterling with the euro.

Poverty trap

Q1 What is the poverty line?

Q2 The main cause of a poverty trap is that people have a right to receive b............... above a level of income at which they start paying t...............

Q3 Why is the implicit rate of taxation highest for poor people caught in the poverty trap?

Q4 Which tax could be introduced to help eliminate the poverty trap?

ANSWERS ▶▶

an overlap which means that poor people start paying tax while they are still entitled to benefits

A1 a level of income below which a person is judged to be in poverty

A2 *benefits*; *tax*; benefits are received while tax is being paid

A3 when they earn additional income they not only pay tax, but also lose the right to claim benefit

A4 a negative or reverse income tax could eliminate the trap caused by a tax–benefit system

***examiner's* note** Because the level at which people start paying tax is the base of the tax pyramid, raising the rate at which people start paying tax will bring about a significant reduction in tax revenue. An alternative to raising the point at which people start paying tax to a level above which they receive benefits is to introduce negative income tax. But this would mean dismantling the benefits system, as the equivalent of welfare payments would be paid as a reverse tax by the Inland Revenue for income not earned.

 ANSWERS

Laffer curve

Q1 What is the optimal tax rate?

Q2 When does a reduction in tax rates benefit politicians?

Q3 Explain why tax falls after T_1.

Q4 Where, on the Laffer curve, was the UK in 1979?

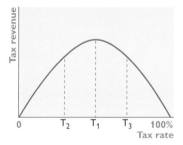

ANSWERS

shows a functional relationship between changes in tax rates and changes in tax revenue

A1 T_1 is the tax rate that produces the highest level of tax revenue

A2 after T_1, politicians can reduce taxes and so gain votes and receive more tax revenue which allows them to spend more and gain even more votes

A3 after T_1, people and firms act to avoid tax as they consider the rates punitive

A4 it is likely that the UK was to the right of T_1, as successive governments have since reduced income and corporation tax rates in the UK

***examiner's* note** The idea put forward by the US economist, Arthur Laffer, could be applied to personal income tax or corporate tax. If people or firms suffer punitive tax rates, they may relocate in foreign countries or reduce their effort. Individuals may decide to substitute leisure for work or pursue tax avoidance schemes, while firms may attempt to shift potential profits into costs and avoid higher taxes.

Counter-cyclical policy

Q1 To what effects is the policy counter-cyclical?

Q2 What characterises a cycle?

Q3 Which policy of the EU is aimed at calming cyclical activity?

Q4 How do Keynesian counter-cyclical policies require fiscal policy to act?

ANSWERS

a strategy to stabilise an economy that opposes the destabilising fluctuation in economic activity

A1   to the damaging effects of changes in economic activity

A2   changes in levels of employment, inflation, economic growth, investment and real GDP

A3   the Stability and Growth Pact

A4   using Keynesian terminology, over-full employment requires a budget surplus, under-full employment a deficit, and full employment a balanced budget

***examiner's* note** There is a debate about whether cyclical activity is a normal side effect of a capitalist economy which will move through boom, recession, depression and recovery, or whether most cyclical activity is caused by the misguided attempts of governments to manage economies about which they have imperfect knowledge. Monetarists state that a steady and stable growth in the money supply will eliminate the main characteristics of cyclical instability.

75 **ANSWERS**

Keynesian economics

Q1 Upon whose principles is Keynesian economics based?

Q2 How is the economy to be fine tuned using fiscal policy under Keynesian economics?

Q3 What are the two main causes of inflation promoted by Keynesian economists?

Q4 What is the multiplier effect of an injection into the economy?

ANSWERS

A1 the economist John Maynard Keynes, who wrote *The General Theory of Employment, Interest and Money* (1936)

A2 using a budget deficit to expand the economy and a budget surplus to reduce excessive demand

A3 demand-pull inflation (at full employment) and cost-push inflation

A4 the economy will expand by an amount greater than the injection

***examiner's* note** Much of Keynes's work offered a new approach to managing the economy. It was argued that, without careful management, the economy could settle at a less than full employment equilibrium or become overheated. Before Keynes, governments were pro-cyclical as a slump meant less spending and a boom more spending. After Keynes, governments acted in a counter-cyclical way and spent more during a slump and less during a boom to reduce the amplitude of the cycle.

Monetarism

Q1 Identify two economists closely associated with the monetarist doctrine.

Q2 Which of the four macroeconomic targets of government does monetarism accept responsibility for?

Q3 What do monetarists say about an efficient monetary policy?

Q4 Is monetarism more often associated with capitalism or communism?

ANSWERS

postulates a relationship between the rate of change in money supply and nominal national income

A1 possible answers include: Irving Fisher; Friedrich Hayek; Milton Friedman

A2 inflation, for which monetarism accepts a role for monetary policy

A3 ideally the money supply grows at the same rate as the real economy, thereby stabilising prices

A4 most monetarists support capitalism as the way to allocate resources

***examiner's* note** It is important to recognise that there is a variable time lag between a change in the money supply and a change in nominal national income. The most contentious prediction of monetarism is that inflation is always and everywhere a monetary phenomenon, where prices rise in response to too much money chasing too few products. In addition, monetarists are often associated with the promotion of free market capitalism and a limited role for government in the allocation of scarce resources.

 **77 ANSWERS**

Comparative advantage

Given the same resources, two countries can produce either quantity of two products:

	Product X	Product Y
Country A	180	150
Country B	90	60

Q1 Which country has absolute advantage in which product(s)?

Q2 What are the opportunity costs of producing one product?

Q3 Wherein lies the comparative advantage?

Q4 For both countries to benefit, at what rate will they trade?

ANSWERS

there will be gains from trade as long as countries have different opportunity costs of production

A1 country A has absolute advantage in the production of both products

A2 country A $1X = (5/6)Y$ or $1Y = (6/5)X$
country B $1X = (2/3)Y$ or $1Y = (3/2)X$

A3 country A has the lowest opportunity cost in product Y and country B in product X

A4 either $1X$ between $(5/6)Y$ and $(2/3)Y$, or $1Y$ between $(6/5)X$ and $(3/2)X$, in order that both countries gain from trade

***examiner's* note** At A-level it is necessary to understand the theory of comparative advantage from the point of view of one country having absolute advantage in the production of both products, but each country having comparative advantage because of the difference in opportunity cost ratios. Although this theory is used to illustrate the gains from trade between countries, it also illustrates why any trade at an internal or international level is beneficial to an economy.

Terms of trade

Q1 What is the difference between terms of trade and a balance of trade?

Q2 What are the real terms of trade?

Q3 Can improvements in the terms of trade worsen the situation on the balance of payments?

Q4 If the index number for exports rises to 117 and for imports to 121, what are the measured terms of trade?

ANSWERS

a measure of how export prices have changed relative to import prices

A1 terms of trade is export prices relative to import prices; a balance of trade is the difference between the total values of exports and imports

A2 the rate at which one country exchanges its surplus product for that of other countries measured in terms of volume rather than price

A3 yes, it depends on the cause of the change in price and the demand elasticity for imports and exports

A4 $\dfrac{117}{121} \times 100 = 96.67$

***examiner's* note** Favourable movements in the terms of trade are shown by a rising figure — this indicates that a country's exports are becoming more expensive relative to its imports. Unfavourable movements are shown by a falling figure — the reverse. However, the overall effect of a favourable change in the terms of trade can, under certain circumstances, worsen the balance on the current account of the balance of payments. This results in a favourable change having an unfavourable effect.

 **ANSWERS**

Exchange rates

Q1 Which labels appear on each axis?

Q2 Why is there only one demand curve?

Q3 Explain why both S and D are determined by demand.

Q4 What is the difference between S, S_1 and S_2?

Sterling exchange rate

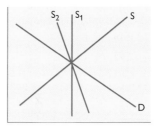

ANSWERS

the price of one currency measured in terms of another currency

A1 the vertical axis can have any currency on it other than sterling; the horizontal axis is the quantity of sterling

A2 the demand for a currency always falls as the price rises and vice versa

A3 S = the demand for imports; D = the demand for exports

A4 S assumes that demand for imports is elastic; S_1 assumes that it is unitary; S_2 assumes that it is inelastic

***examiner's* note** A common mistake is to put a sterling sign on the vertical axis; you can only measure the price of sterling in terms of another currency. It is also important to recognise that the usual upward-sloping supply curve (S) is based on an assumption of elastic demand for imports. It is quite possible that demand for imports could be inelastic (S_2) or even unitary (S_1). To understand this, it is useful to refer back to your AS notes on elasticity and what happens to revenue as price changes.

Floating exchange rate

Q1 Which acronym is commonly used to represent the foreign exchange market?

Q2 What determines the supply of currency to the foreign exchange market?

Q3 In a floating exchange rate market, what will happen if people in the UK increase their demand for foreign holidays?

Q4 What is the likely effect of a rise in interest rates in the UK on the sterling exchange rate?

ANSWERS

the price of a currency is determined by, and changes as a result of, market forces

A1 FOREX

A2 the demand for imports

A3 there will be an increase in the supply of currency to the FOREX market and the sterling exchange rate will fall

A4 an increase in demand for UK assets will raise the exchange rate

***examiner's* note** When explaining the determination of an exchange rate in a free market, remember that the price of one currency can only be measured in terms of another currency. Therefore, when drawing a graph of the price of sterling, the vertical axis must read dollars or another currency. It is a common mistake for students to place a sterling sign on the vertical axis to represent the price of sterling. Remember too that the supply of and the demand for sterling are determined by the demand for imports and exports.

Fixed exchange rate

Q1 Do market forces act in this market?

Q2 Why are fixed exchange rates variable within specified limits?

Q3 What will happen if the exchange rate is likely to fall below its lower limit?

Q4 What is the difference between revaluation and appreciation of a currency?

ANSWERS

an agreed rate at which the price of the domestic currency is to be sustained against other currencies

A1 yes, supply and demand determine the exchange rate and there is intervention buying and selling of the currency

A2 there is insufficient knowledge to be able to buy and sell currency in a way that will totally fix the price

A3 the government will sell foreign currency and buy domestic currency to raise its price

A4 revaluation is the term used when a fixed exchange rate is fixed at a higher value, while appreciation refers to floating upwards

***examiner's* note** Both fixed and floating exchange rates are determined by market forces. The only difference is that, with a fixed rate, government has made an overt statement that its agent will intervene in the market and buy and sell the currency, using its reserves, to maintain an agreed range of prices around a central target value.

Managed float

Q1 What is the difference between a free float and a managed float?

Q2 What is 'smoothing the trend'?

Q3 Which agency manages the float, from what source is it managed and on which account is it recorded?

Q4 Why may the government be more concerned about the change from $1.01/£1 to $0.99/£1 than from $1.49/£1 to $1.39/£1?

ANSWERS ⟩⟩

market forces are the main determinant of the exchange rate, but government may intervene

A1 a free float involves market forces and no intervention, while a managed float involves market forces with government intervention

A2 where a government acts in a counter-cyclical way to reduce the extremes of exchange rate changes

A3 the Bank of England; foreign exchange reserves; the Exchange Equalisation Account

A4 going through the boundary from 1 to 0 is politically sensitive and likely to produce a press reaction

***examiner's* note** It is difficult to manage a float unless the underlying trend of exchange rate change is recognised. If the trend is down, it is unwise to try and manage the float upwards, as sooner or later the exchange rate will have to be brought into line with the market value of the currency.

International trade barriers

Q1 Identify three types of trade barrier.

Q2 Identify two economic reasons for imposing a trade barrier.

Q3 Does a tariff shift the supply curve for imports to the right or left?

Q4 What is the difference between barriers erected by customs unions and free trade areas?

ANSWERS ▶▶

restrictions on the free movement of products between countries

A1 tariffs; quotas; legal restrictions; differential tax rates

A2 infant industry; dumping; unfair or illegal activities

A3 to the left, as it acts in the same way as a rise in the costs of production

A4 customs union members are protected by a common external tariff; members of a free trade area each have their own barriers against other countries

***examiner's* note** Many other types of trade barriers are introduced for non-economic reasons. Although it is possible that there may be a short-term benefit from introducing a trade barrier, it is unlikely that this effect will last in the long term. If the barrier interferes with free trade, it is likely to impose inefficiency on resource allocation and this is liable to be worsened when other countries retaliate by raising their own barriers.

Devaluation

Q1 What is the difference between devaluation and depreciation?

Q2 What effect does devaluation have on the sterling price of domestic products and imports?

Q3 What condition of the current account of the balance of payments is likely to lead to devaluation of the currency?

Q4 What is the j-curve effect?

ANSWERS

the reduction in the par value of one currency to a lower fixed level against other currencies

A1 devaluation takes place under a fixed exchange rate system; depreciation occurs under a floating system

A2 the sterling price of domestic products is unchanged but the sterling price of imports rises

A3 a persistent deficit where the value of imported products is greater than the value of exported products

A4 the situation that occurs after a devaluation when there is an immediate worsening of the current balance before it starts to improve

***examiner's* note** A devaluation has the immediate effect of lowering export prices and raising import prices on the current level of sales, thus worsening the current balance. Over the longer term, and dependent upon elasticity, the volume and value of exports increase and those of imports decrease.

Balance of payments disequilibrium

Q1 What is the difference between a deficit and a disequilibrium?

Q2 Disequilibrium on which account is of most concern?

Q3 Which disequilibrium is most common on the current account of the UK balance of payments?

Q4 Which two macroeconomic policies can be used to deal with a persistent surplus on the current account, given a fixed exchange rate?

ANSWERS

a fundamental imbalance between the current, capital or financial flows

A1 a deficit means that outflows are greater than inflows;
a disequilibrium can be a deficit or a surplus

A2 disequilibrium on the current account

A3 the UK current balance is more often than not in deficit

A4 revaluing the currency or reflating domestic demand

***examiner's* note** Questions about disequilibrium are often answered by
reference to a deficit on the current account of the balance of payments. It it
important to note that a surplus is also a disequilibrium. Given a surplus, there is
potential to increase the flow of imports and raise living standards, but one
country's surplus is matched by deficits in other countries, and pressure may be
applied to the surplus country to revalue, appreciate or reflate.

Marshall–Lerner condition

Q1 Does a UK devaluation change the sterling price of exports?

Q2 If there is a current balance deficit and the sum of the demand elasticities is less than one, should a country devalue or revalue?

Q3 What will be the change in demand for exports if sterling is devalued by 5% and elasticity is 0.25?

Q4 What will be the change in demand for imports if sterling is devalued by 5% and elasticity is 0.75?

ANSWERS

for a devaluation to succeed, the sum of demand elasticities for X and M must be greater than unity

A1 no, only the foreign currency price changes (a fall for a devaluation)

A2 revaluation will reduce the size of the deficit

A3 a rise of 1.25%

A4 a fall of 3.75%

***examiner's* note** The sum of demand elasticities in questions 3 and 4 adds up to unity. A devaluation of 5% will raise demand for and revenue from export sales by 1.25%. The price of imports rises by 5% and sales fall by 3.75%, leading to an increase in expenditure on imports of 1.25%. Both spending on imports and exports rises by the same percentage if the sum of the elasticities is equal to one.

Expenditure dampening/switching

Q1 Which macroeconomic problem do expenditure dampening and switching policies aim to overcome?

Q2 Distinguish between the policies used for dampening expenditure and those concerned with switching expenditure.

Q3 Is revaluation of the exchange rate dampening or switching?

Q4 If there is a current balance deficit when the economy is inflating past the point of full employment, which policy would be more effective?

ANSWERS ▶▶

A1 a persistent deficit on the current account of the balance of payments

A2 deflating domestic demand is a dampening policy, while changing the external value of the currency is a switching policy

A3 revaluation raises the price of exports and reduces the price of imports and is therefore a switching policy

A4 a dampening policy will help control inflation and improve a current balance problem

***examiner's* note** There is a problem in choosing whether to use dampening or switching policies to manage the balance of payments, since there is a debate among economists about what is meant by a fully employed economy and the extent to which it is possible to manipulate aggregate demand and stimulate or control the level of economic activity.

Euro

Q1 What is the difference between a fixed exchange rate and a single European currency?

Q2 Is exchange rate policy available to members of the eurozone?

Q3 Which organisation administers monetary policy for the eurozone countries?

Q4 'The euro provides traders with transparency.' What does this mean?

ANSWERS ▶▶

A1 a fixed exchange rate ties together separate currencies;
the euro replaces separate currencies

A2 yes, but only to all eurozone countries combined, not
to individual members

A3 the European Central Bank (ECB)

A4 prices are all denominated in the same currency in different
countries so it is easy to identify price differences

examiner's note Countries within the eurozone can still manage their own
fiscal policies, but they cannot determine monetary or exchange rate policy
independently — these are managed by the ECB. The euro is supported by
traders who value transparency and the fact that there are no transaction costs
caused by the need for currency conversion. Some politicians are more sceptical
about the loss of control.

European Central Bank (ECB)

Q1 What is the structure of the ECB?

Q2 How does the ECB inflation target differ from the Bank of England inflation target?

Q3 What is the difference between the ESCB and the ECB?

Q4 The ECB uses both i.............. r.............. and m.............. t.............. to achieve its goals.

ANSWERS

the central bank of the eurozone area which manages the supply and price of the euro

A1 the Governing Council of the ECB includes the governors of all the central banks of eurozone countries

A2 the ECB target is 2% or below using the HICP; the Bank of England target is 2% +/–1% using the CPI

A3 the European System of Central Banks (ESCB) includes the national banks of all EU members; the ECB is the central bank for the eurozone

A4 *interest rates; monetary targets*

***examiner's* note** The ECB oversees a number of countries and is not accountable to anyone other than itself; in contrast, the Bank of England pursues UK monetary policy and is accountable to the UK government, which sets the targets. The ECB pursues EU policies, conducts foreign currency operations and manages the official foreign exchange reserves of the euro member countries.

Globalisation

Q1 What is the difference between globalisation and trade liberalisation?

Q2 Which aspect of communication media has accelerated the pace of globalisation?

Q3 The free movement of labour throughout the EU creates a more efficient d.............. of l.............. .

Q4 Globalisation is restrained by the threat of t.............. .

ANSWERS

the development of a supranational economy in the markets for products, assets and productive factors

A1 globalisation embraces free movement of people, ideas and products and is therefore more than just liberalising trade

A2 the internet

A3 *division; labour*

A4 *terrorism*

***examiner's* note** The internet is breaking down national barriers as it allows people to communicate and trade outside limited geographical boundaries. It is relatively easy to explore virtual markets, place orders for CDs in Hong Kong, book flights in Australia, hotels in Alaska and tickets for football matches in Spain. There are also dangers with globalisation, as extremist groups can flourish. It is therefore important that internet and international laws are developed to protect human rights throughout the world.

 **91 ANSWERS**

Lorenz curve

Q1 What is on the axes AB and AD?

Q2 What does the straight line AC imply?

Q3 If the shaded area is 8 and ABCD is 64, what is the Gini coefficient?

Q4 What is the Gini coefficient of absolute inequality?

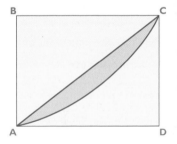

ANSWERS ▶▶

a visual representation of income inequality in a country

A1 AB is cumulative percentage of total income; AD is cumulative percentage of population

A2 that there is perfect equality of income across the population

A3 the Gini coefficient is the shaded area 8 divided by the triangle ACD (which is 64 ÷ 2 = 32): 8 ÷ 32 = 0.25

A4 1, as the equivalent of the shaded area would be the triangle ACD

***examiner's* note** More economically developed countries tend to have a more equal distribution of income with a Gini coefficient which is nearer to zero than that of less economically developed countries. In less economically developed countries there is usually an absence of middle income earners, with some very rich and many very poor people. Over time it is expected that most countries will develop more equality of income.

European Union (EU)

Q1 In 1957 the EEC was set up as a customs union. Was this a step towards freer or more protected trade?

Q2 Which industry in the EU is given special privileges and protected by minimum price guarantees?

Q3 Name five members who joined the EU in May 2004.

Q4 Which event is considered to be the most significant in creating single market status for member countries?

ANSWERS

a group of countries having free trade, common policies and a common external tariff

A1 freer trade — barriers were lowered against the rest of the world and eliminated between members

A2 the agricultural industry with its common agricultural policy (CAP)

A3 Hungary; Malta; Czech Republic; Slovakia; Lithuania; Estonia; Slovenia; Cyprus; Poland; Latvia

A4 the acceptance of a single European currency (euro)

***examiner's* note** Originally established as a customs union, the EEC quickly developed into an integrated political unit with common policies for transport, agriculture and other important industries, as well as a legislative programme and a social charter. The gradual movement towards a single European market was helped by the introduction of the euro as a single currency which gave transparency to pricing decisions. As yet, the UK considers adopting the euro currency a step too far.

Single European market

Q1 What was the aim of the Single European Act of 1987?

Q2 In the context of the EU, what is the difference between a customs union and a single market?

Q3 In a single large market firms should be able to take advantage of e................... of s...................

Q4 What step does the UK need to take in order to become more integrated into a single market?

ANSWERS

no barriers to trade or the movement
of productive factors; political, legal and
social cohesion

A1 to mould individual member countries of the EU into a single, indivisible free market

A2 a customs union involves the free flow of products; the single market adds the free movement of productive factors

A3 *economies; scale*

A4 it needs to join the eurozone and accept the euro as its currency

***examiner's* note** Since the Single European Act of 1987 there has been significant movement towards achieving a single European market. Trade barriers are down and labour has been able to move freely throughout Europe.

Trade liberalisation

Q1 Why is trade liberalisation important to economists?

Q2 Which international body is particularly concerned with trade liberalisation?

Q3 Why is the CAP of the EU seen to be against trade liberalisation?

Q4 When is the establishment of a customs union beneficial to trade liberalisation?

ANSWERS

the process of reducing trade barriers throughout the world

A1 to take advantage of the benefits from free trade and comparative advantage

A2 the World Trade Organisation (WTO) which has taken over from the General Agreement on Tariffs and Trade (GATT)

A3 it limits trade through import levies and export subsidies

A4 when the overall effect is a reduction in trade barriers

***examiner's* note** In the case of the EU and its forerunner the EEC, the founding principle which reduced trade barriers was the agreement to trade freely between members and erect a common external tariff that was the lowest of the founding countries. If there is already free trade between a group of countries and the rest of the world, then the setting up of a customs union is likely to impose an overall restraint on trade.

International Bank for Reconstruction and Development (IBRD)

Q1 Which other international organisation was set up in 1945 alongside the IBRD?

Q2 What was the original brief of the IBRD and what is its current brief?

Q3 Identify two services offered by the IBRD.

Q4 How does the IBRD finance its activities?

ANSWERS

A1 the International Monetary Fund (IMF)

A2 the original brief was postwar reconstruction; the current brief is to support economic development in member countries with a particular emphasis on developing countries

A3 loans for capital projects; academic institutes; advice and training; project feasibility and evaluation studies

A4 from contributions made by member countries

***examiner's* note** The World Bank has the advantage of being able to carry out its activities without being restricted by the rules and regulations imposed by individual countries. In general, its lending rates are low and stable, although they are subject to a quarterly review. The Bank provides and coordinates a wide range of technical and other programmes of assistance. It also runs the Economic Development Institute which provides education and training for government officials of member countries.

Environmental degradation

Q1 Which resources are threatened by environmental degradation?

Q2 What is the 'greenhouse effect'?

Q3 It is argued that p.................. p.................. r..................
are more likely to protect the environment than the
common ownership of land.

Q4 Which mechanism do enthusiasts of the free market
argue will do most to help solve the problem of
degradation?

ANSWERS ⟩⟩

a decline in the quality of the environment as a result of economic activities

A1 non-renewable resources

A2 the result of a build-up of carbon dioxide and other industrial pollutants in the atmosphere that is causing global warming

A3 *private property rights*

A4 they argue that the price mechanism will allocate resources efficiently by rationing use and prompting the development of substitutes

***examiner's* note** There is much debate about whether environmental degradation is the result of a ruthless exploitation of resources by greedy capitalists or whether it is the result of a failure to establish private property rights and impose national and international laws. National laws protect the environment and international laws deal with problems caused by stretches of land in common ownership or confused ownership, e.g. overfishing and whaling in the oceans and destruction of the hardwood forests.

 ANSWERS

Foreign aid

Q1 Identify three different types of foreign aid.

Q2 What is the main economic advantage that less developed countries have over more developed countries?

Q3 Why do a number of less developed countries back the slogan 'trade not aid'?

Q4 Why may foreign direct investment (FDI) provide a better solution than foreign aid to less developed countries?

ANSWERS

transfers from more developed countries to less developed ones to support economic development

A1 long-term loans; soft loans; technical help; charitable gifts

A2 cheaper labour costs, particularly for unskilled forms of employment

A3 trade provides a long-term solution and requires the more developed countries to provide free access to their markets

A4 FDI provides long-term jobs and income, whereas aid is uncertain and variable

***examiner's* note** Most people agree that in the long term less developed countries would be best served if the more developed world removed the barriers that prevent price competition and a free flow of trade. The EU's Common Agricultural Policy is often cited as an example of the kind of barrier less economically developed countries face when entering a market.

Harrod–Domar growth model

Q1 Define economic growth.

Q2 Can economic growth take place when all resources are fully employed?

Q3 What was Rostow's growth model?

Q4 What is the accelerator investment function in the Harrod–Domar model?

ANSWERS ▶▶

one of the earliest growth models developed in the 1940s around an accelerator investment function

A1 an increase in productive capacity per capita

A2 yes, as an increase in the efficiency with which resources are used can shift the production possibility frontier outwards

A3 it incorporated the five stages of growth from traditional society — preconditions for takeoff, takeoff, maturity and mass production and consumption

A4 investment is a function of a change in national income and is often considered to be a precondition of a boom in the trade cycle

examiner's note A number of economists have investigated, with limited success, what causes an economy to grow. Rostow's attempt produced a reasonably descriptive model, while the Harrod–Domar model introduced a more rigorous analysis based on an accelerator investment function.

 ANSWERS

Human development index (HDI)

Q1 Why is the HDI a better measure of standard of living than real GDP?

Q2 Identify two other characteristics of standard of living not included in HDI.

Q3 Identify two problems associated with comparing living standards in one country over time.

Q4 Identify two problems associated with comparing living standards between countries.

ANSWERS ▶▶

a comparative measure of quality of life using per capita income, life expectancy and literacy rates

A1 it includes additional variables to real GDP and adds per capita to the measure

A2 political freedom; stability; security; scenery

A3 how and for how long the relevant statistics have been collected; changes in money value, distributions of income and wealth, externalities, quality of the product

A4 population statistics and how they are collected; differences in currencies, exchange rate, purchasing power parity, non-marketed resources, working hours, defence budget

examiner's note Standard of living comparisons often form the basis of exam questions. Read the question carefully and make sure you are clear whether the comparison is over time, across borders or both.